EXPORT MANAGEMENT

STRATEGIES FOR GLOBAL SUCCESS

DR. JAGADEESH PILLAI

‖ Dedicated to all wisdom seekers around the world ‖

Contents

Contents

Prayer

"Om Bhadram Karnebhih Shrunuyaama
DevaahBhadram Pashyemaakshabhiryajatraah
SthirairangaistushtuvaamsastanoobhihVyashema
Devahitam YadaayuhSwasti Na Indro
VridhashravaahSwasti Nah Pooshaa
VishwavedaahSwasti Nastaarkshyo ArishtanemihSwasti
No Brihaspatir DadhaatuOm Shantih, Shantih, Shantih"

The literal meaning of this mantra is: OM. O Gods! Let us hear auspicious words from our ears. O reverent Gods! Let us behold propitious visions from our eyes, let our organs and body be stable, healthy, and strong. Let us do that which is pleasing to the gods in the life span allotted to us. May Indra, inscribed in the scriptures, bring us fortune! May Pushan, the knower of the world, grant us prosperity! May Trakshya, who vanquishes enemies, bestow us with blessings! May Brihaspati bring us success!
OM Peace, Peace, Peace.

About The Author

Dr. Jagadeesh Pillai is a renowned Guinness World Record holder, writer, and researcher hailing from Varanasi, also known as the abode of Lord Shiva. With a Ph.D. in Vedic Science and a range of creative ideas and achievements, he is a true polymath. He is the author of more than 100 books including Research Publications. Although his roots can be traced back to Kerala, the people of Varanasi hold him in high regard and affectionately consider him one of their own.

In 1998, Dr. Pillai was offered a job at Banaras Hindu University, but he left the position after only two months to pursue greater goals in life. He believed that in order to study Indian scriptures and engage in other creative endeavours, he needed to retire from the daily grind of working solely for money at a young age.

He started an export business from scratch, using the knowledge he had gained from a previous job in the industry. His intelligence and unique approach to business led to great success in a short period of time, earning him more in just a decade and a half than he would have in a lifetime working in a government job. Upon the passing of Dr. APJ Abdul Kalam, Dr. Pillai decided to leave the business and dedicate himself to reading, studying, researching, and experimenting.

During his tenure in the export business, Dr. Pillai traveled to over 16 countries, gaining valuable insight and experiencing the world and life in detail.

Dr. Pillai has achieved four Guinness World Records in the following subjects:

"Script to Screen" - In this record, Dr. Pillai produced and directed an animation film within the shortest time possible, breaking the previous record set by Canadians. He has also received numerous national and international awards and recognitions for this achievement.

Longest Line of Postcards - For this record, Dr. Pillai created a line of 16,300 postcards on the occasion of the 163rd anniversary of Indian Postal Day. The event also included a questionnaire about the Indian flag.

Largest Poster Awareness Campaign - Dr. Pillai designed an awareness campaign on the subject of "Beti Bachao - Beti Padhao" (Save the Girl Child - Educate the Girl Child) to achieve this record.

Largest Envelope - In tribute to the Indian Prime Minister's "Make in India" initiative, Dr. Pillai created a 4000 square meter envelope using waste paper to achieve this record.

Attempted - **70000 Candles on a 210 kg Cake** - To celebrate the 70th Indian Independence Day, Dr. Pillai attempted to light 70,000 candles on a 210 kg cake, which was recorded in World Records India.

Attempted - **Documentary on Dhamek Stupa of Sarnath in 17 Languages** - Dr. Pillai attempted to create a documentary on the Dhamek Stupa of Sarnath, dubbing it in 17 different languages. The result of this attempt is currently awaiting confirmation from the Guinness World Records.

Dr. Pillai is skilled in teaching the Bhagavad Gita, a Hindu scripture, and is popular among young people. He has helped many young people improve their lives through his motivational teachings.

In addition to teaching, he has composed and sung numerous Sanskrit Bhajans and patriotic songs.

He has also written and directed several short films and documentaries for awareness campaigns, and has volunteered with the police in both UP and Kerala to spread awareness about various issues through videos and photography.

Incredibly, he has produced and directed over 100 documentaries about the city of Varanasi, all on his own.

He has also helped and guided more than 25 boys and girls to achieve world records through creative and innovative methods. He is a multifaceted person who uses his intellect and the blessings given to him by God to excel in various areas. He is both a teacher and a student, always learning and teaching, and is able to master any subject he comes across.

He is a selfless social activist and motivational speaker who has overcome struggles and failures to become a successful and enthusiastic individual with a rich life experience.

In addition to his work with the Bhagavad Gita, he is also

an efficient Tarot card reader, Astro-Vastu consultant, and a talented singer and composer. He has sung the entire Ram Charita Manas and Bhagavad Gita in his own compositions, and has sung the phrase "Lokah Samastha Sukhino Bhavantu" in 50 different languages. He is currently working on a detailed and scientific study of Vedas, Upanishads, Puranas, and the Bhagavad Gita. He has also composed and sung the Hanuman Chalisa and Gayatri Mantra in 108 and 1008 different compositions, respectively.

Awards - Four Times Guinness World Records, Winner of Mahatma Gandhi Vishwa Shanti Puraskar, Mahatma Gandhi Global Peace Ambassador, Kashi Ratna Award, Dr. APJ Abdul Kalam Motivational Person of the Year 2017, Mother Teresa Award, Indira Gandhi Priyadarshini Award, Bharat Vikas Ratna Award, Udyog Ratna Award, Vigyan Prasar Award, Poorvanchal Ratn Samman.

Preface

Export Management: Strategies for Global Success is an essential guide for MBA students looking to gain the knowledge and skills needed to succeed in the ever-changing world of international trade and business. This book provides a comprehensive overview of the strategies and tools required to build a successful export business.

Through a combination of case studies and real-world examples, students will gain a deep understanding of how to develop, manage, and expand their export operations. Additionally, this book delves into essential topics such as global economics, international finance, legal considerations, and export logistics. By the end of this book, MBA students will be equipped with the essential knowledge and skills to confidently and effectively facilitate successful export operations.

With this book, students will gain the confidence and expertise to navigate the complexities of international trade and business, and ultimately achieve global success.

CHAPTER ONE

Introduction to Export Management

An introduction to export management is essential for any business looking to expand their operations into international markets. Export management involves the coordination of activities related to the sale of goods and services to customers in foreign countries. It requires a comprehensive understanding of the legal, financial, and logistical aspects of international trade.

Export management involves a range of activities, from researching potential markets and customers to negotiating contracts and shipping goods. It also involves staying up-to-date on the latest regulations and trends in international trade. Companies must be aware of the different cultural, political, and economic factors that can affect their export operations.

Successful export management requires a thorough understanding of the global marketplace and the ability to develop effective strategies for entering new markets. Companies must be able to identify potential customers, develop marketing plans, and negotiate contracts. They must also be able to manage the logistics of shipping goods and services to foreign countries.

Export management is a complex and ever-evolving field. Companies must stay abreast of the latest developments in international trade and be prepared to adjust their strategies accordingly. With the right knowledge and expertise, businesses can take advantage of the many opportunities available in the global marketplace.

CHAPTER TWO

Globalization and the International Business Environment

Globalization and international business have become an integral part of the business environment. It has allowed businesses to expand their reach and scope, while also giving customers access to a large selection of products and services. Furthermore, globalization has made competition among businesses more fierce than ever before.

Globalization has meant that businesses now have access to larger markets, allowing them to reach more customers and tap into greater opportunities than ever before. As global trade increases, it further encourages global investment and business opportunities. This increased competition helps businesses become more innovative and efficient. For example, a business may lack the resources to succeed in its domestic market but can take advantage of international markets where the same resources are available more cheaply and in greater quantities.

Globalization has also led to the creation of a more integrated business environment. Companies can now access a host of services from any corner of the world, allowing them to create more efficient, scaled-up operations. It has also led to the development of global business practices and universal standards of production. This allows businesses to leverage the advantages of economies of scale, further enhancing business efficiency.

Moreover, international business has also seen a rise in the number of international partnerships and collaborations, which has helped to create a more open business environment. Companies have been able to develop closer relationships with their international counterparts and even form joint ventures, allowing them to create a global presence. Moreover, international collaborations also help business to benefit from the synergies created by different businesses.

Finally, globalization has helped to create a more dynamic business environment, with businesses now able to quickly adjust to changing economic conditions due to the increased flexibility provided by international collaboration. By taking advantage of an international network of businesses, companies can quickly shift strategies and adapt quickly to trends and customer demand in order to stay ahead of the competition.

Overall, globalization and international business have brought great benefits for both businesses and customers. By allowing companies to expand their presence and tap into international markets, globalization and international business have transformed the business environment and provided opportunities for businesses to reach new heights.

Cultural Intelligence and Cross-cultural Management

Cultural intelligence and cross-cultural management are two essential elements to help a business succeed in today's globally interconnected marketplace. Cultural intelligence (CQ) is the ability to flexibly interact with people from different cultures, while cross-cultural management is the set of management strategies, techniques and methods to addressing the cross-cultural needs of employees, customers, and other stakeholders in a globalized business setting.

To begin, let's first examine cultural intelligence and how it can benefit a business. A successful business needs the ability to effectively communicate, navigate and navigate cultural differences. Understanding the experiences, values, and beliefs of people from other cultures is a key part of this. When a business has a high CQ, it is able to better interpret the behavior of their customers and employees, enabling them to offer better services, products and engagement opportunities.

Cross-cultural management is another essential piece of the puzzle. A successful cross-cultural management strategy can provide the overarching guidance needed to foster trust, understanding and collaboration across cultures, teams, and departments. This strategy is especially important for businesses operating in a multi-cultural setting, allowing them to create a single corporate culture that everyone shares.

When both cultural intelligence and cross-cultural management are successfully integrated, a business can reap the rewards of increased efficiency, better diversity of thought and experience, and improved team morale. Furthermore, when all stakeholders understand the cross-cultural dynamics within a business, ideas and perspectives from many different backgrounds are better included, leading to higher levels of innovation.

In order to maximize the effectiveness of a business's cultural intelligence and cross-cultural management, employees must be well-trained in both. Training should include instruction on how to interpret and adapt to cultural cues, and how to navigate common miscommunication. Additionally, businesses should look to reward employees who demonstrate high levels of cultural sensitivity and understanding. This can include special rewards and recognition, as well as promotions.

Cultural intelligence and cross-cultural management are two of the essential components to a business's success in today's globalized marketplace. Companies that are equipped with the right strategies and understand how to effectively use them will be better able to harness the creativity and insight of employees from all backgrounds. When a business has a high CQ and a well-crafted cross-cultural management strategy, it will be one step closer to becoming a fully globalized and culturally competent business.

CHAPTER FOUR

International Market Research and Analysis

International market research and analysis is a fundamental aspect of business management. As an MBA student, understanding and using market research is imperative to success. International Market research involves gathering data from different sources and leveraging it to gain a better understanding of potential markets, customers' expectations, consumer behavior, and industry trends. Understanding these factors gives businesses the potential to make informed decisions and set realistic goals.

One of the most important elements of international market research and analysis is determining the size and scope of a potential market. Additionally, researchers must understand how different marketing strategies are tailored to different cultures and customer preferences. Gathering customer feedback through surveys, focus groups, and interviews can provide further insight on market opportunities and customer expectations.

From this data, market analysts create models for pricing, customer service, and other factors based on current and projected statistics. Market analysts then interpret and report the data in the form of graphs, tables, and presentations. Employing market research and analysis can help businesses identify potential flaws in existing strategies, understand competitive advantages needed to succeed in the global market, and develop effective strategies for entering new markets.

Data-driven analytics can assist businesses in understanding the competitive environment and leverage resources. For example, businesses can use analytics to assess current and future marketing campaigns, analyze customer behavior, and adjust to changing international markets. Such analytics provide the information necessary to build a successful international business strategy.

By combining market research and analysis with analytical tools, businesses can maximize their impact in the global market. With this data, companies can assess and react to customer opinions, identify new opportunities, and devise projects that appeal to international customers. With the right tools, businesses can gain a competitive edge in the global market and position themselves for success. International market research and analysis is critical to the success of any business and indispensable to modern MBA graduates.

CHAPTER FIVE

International Marketing and Branding

The business world of today is ever-evolving and highly competitive. As a result, area of Marketing and Branding is one of utmost importance every organization needs to pay attention to. In the context of international marketing and branding though, the challenges and opportunities can be even greater and more wide-ranging.

International marketing and branding involves marketing and branding products and services to customers in more than one country. It requires grappling with the various cultural, legal, political, and economic factors in each international market. It involves careful consideration of local trends and customs and how they fit into an organization's overall global strategy. There are nuances that can be very different in each country. So, there is a lot to learn in international marketing and branding. Fortunately, though, there are invaluable lessons that can be drawn from an MBA program in marketing and branding to equip you with the knowledge and skills needed to succeed in this field.

At the core of any MBA program in marketing and branding, you will learn basic marketing principles, such as segmentation, targeting and positioning. You will also learn about pricing strategies and research methods for understanding customer behavior. You will be taught about advertising, public relations and product promotion. All of these fundamental components need to be taken into account in international marketing and branding.

The biggest challenge in international marketing and branding is achieving a consistent but differentiated brand across different countries. Each country will have a unique cultural context, different preferences and different tastes for specific products. As such, an organization needs to be able to identify these country/region-specific needs, create an effective brand image, and employ strategies that align with them. To do so, you will need to understand the different dynamics in each international market and be able to adjust your strategies accordingly. This is where MBA programs in marketing and branding can come in. They can provide the training and the knowledge to make well-informed decisions while marketing and promoting international goods and services.

Finally, MBA programs in marketing and branding offer invaluable insights into current trends in the field. It offers the chance to learn from research, guest speakers and practitioners with first-hand experience. Research on important topics like digital marketing, A.I. and social media marketing can prove crucial for staying ahead of the curve.

All in all, MBA programs in marketing and branding

provide the necessary tools to succeed in international marketing and branding. They make it possible to reach customers from across the globe and create a unified but differentiated brand. This is pivotal for any organization striving to stay ahead in today's competitive global marketplace.

CHAPTER SIX

International Sales and Distribution

International sales and distribution is fundamentally the process of selling a company's goods or services to global markets and then transporting and delivering the products to foreign consumers, clients, and partners alike. Managing a successful international sales and distribution system requires a deep understanding of the nuances that go into selling across a diverse range of cultures, languages, and levels of economic development. All are factors which influence every detail of the export process, right down to logistics and customer service.

The first step in export management is to thoroughly research foreign markets and potential customers. Different countries have different import regulations, product standards, and business practices, and a successful business must analyze these factors to ensure their products, services, and message can reach the intended audience. Investing in the appropriate market studies, audits and market visits is necessary to understand the complexity of an international market. Once a target market is identified and understood, a company must set up a network of international distributors and sales representatives to target customers in those markets. Negotiating and signing a non-exclusive distribution agreement can be a lengthy, detail-oriented process, but it must be done in order to have a successful presence in the international marketplace.

Ensuring goods are packaged and shipped in compliance with international standards is also key before making a sale. Transport goods must also be properly taken care of—documents must be drafted, orders must be packed, and products must be handled properly. There are also certain responsibilities that must be negotiated between the seller and the importer, both of which must adhere to any relevant international trade laws.

Logistics is the last piece of the puzzle in international sales and distribution. FINDING, contracting, and managing freight forwarders, third-party logistics companies and other transport service providers is not only expensive, but it must be done properly to ensure the goods reach their destination in a timely and cost-effective manner. Once the goods arrive, there might be duties, taxes and other fees associated with the delivery and must be taken into consideration when pricing a product.

In summary, a successful international sales and distribution strategy requires a comprehensive understanding of international buyers, compliance with international standards and regulations, and a comprehensive logistics and transportation network. Companies that do their research, properly plan, develop their network, and stay up to date on the nuances of international trade stand to benefit greatly from their international sales and distribution investments.

CHAPTER SEVEN

International Pricing and Promotion

International pricing and promotion are essential marketing strategies for a successful business operating in multiple countries. Any company selling a product or service outside of its home market needs to understand the local regulations, customs and preferences of each market. The application of international pricing and promotion within the global economy is increasingly important for the success of any business hoping to gain a competitive edge.

When deciding how to price and promote a product or service to a foreign market, there are several considerations to bear in mind. First, it must be taken into account the local laws and standards governing sales and promotions. Many countries have strict rules regarding discounts, labelling and advertising. Business owners must be aware of these rules and adapt their sales strategies accordingly.

Second, there is the cultural aspect to take into account. Different countries have different values and ways of thinking, so promotional messages must be tailored to each country's particular needs and expectations. For example, what may be deemed acceptable in one country may not be in another.

Third, the company must be aware of the local currency exchange rate, and how that affects the purchasing power of the consumers. Companies should adjust their prices to make them competitive in each local market. For example, currency exchange rates might make a product more appealing in a certain country, so the company will have to adjust its pricing structure to capture those sales.

Finally, the company must decide what type of promotional activities will be effective in the foreign market. Different countries have different preferences when it comes to marketing. For example, some countries rely heavily on TV and radio advertisements, while others prefer digital marketing campaigns. Knowing these local customs, as well as creating innovative promotional activities, can greatly increase sales.

Overall, international pricing and promotions are an important part of any company's international business strategy. To be successful, companies must be aware of the local laws, customs and preferences of the foreign markets in which they are operating. They must also understand the local currency exchange rates and be able to craft effective promotional activities. By taking all of these factors into consideration, companies can increase their sales and gain a competitive edge in the global market.

CHAPTER EIGHT

Product Development for Export Markets

Product development for export markets is a critical component of any successful international business. It requires an understanding of both the customer's needs, and the cultural and legal requirements of the country in which they are located. Companies must take into account the needs and wants of their customer base, while simultaneously accounting for the necessary compliance considerations.

The first step in successful product development for export markets is understanding customer needs. This involves researching the local customer base, studying customer preferences, and understanding how competitors are successfully catering to the needs of customers in the local market. Companies should identify any potential demands that their product can meet, and build upon them. Companies must also research and familiarise themselves with the local customer's industry and the tastes and preferences of local consumers. Companies should then create a product that is tailored to the local customer base and which has the potential to be a success in the foreign market.

An equally important step in successful product development for export markets is developing a product that is compliant with the laws, regulations and cultural norms of the target country. It is important to note that these can vary greatly between countries, leading to the need for extensive research. Companies should research the laws and regulations that must be followed in order to launch the product in the target country. It is also important to understand the local culture and develop a product that does not contradict cultural norms. Companies should also create a product that meets all safety standards and is approved for sale or distribution in the target country.

Finally, successful product development for export markets often involves creating a product that can access and benefit from any international export incentives or trade agreements. Companies should do due diligence to research which international economic agreements exist between the target country and other countries which can be leveraged, such as the Common Market for Eastern and Southern Africa. These agreements provide great opportunities for companies to lower costs and maximize their profits.

To successfully develop a product for export markets, companies must understand local customer needs and create a product that caters to them, is compliant with the laws and regulations of the country and makes the most of any relevant international trade agreements. If these considerations are adequately researched and incorporated, then companies can create a successful new product that can successfully be launched and sold in foreign markets.

CHAPTER NINE

Foreign Direct Investment and Mergers and Acquisitions

Foreign direct investment (FDI) and mergers and acquisitions (M&A) are two of the strongest drivers of export strategies for multinational corporations. FDI, or direct investment in one company's ownership or equity in another company, is a particularly powerful tool for export strategies since it provides the opportunity for firms to build new operations in foreign markets or access new technologies to improve their competitiveness. Mergers and acquisitions, on the other hand, refer to the process of combining two or more business entities into a single organization and can be used as a form of FDI as one company may acquire another. Such strategies are typically innovative as they provide a global reach that can help secure new markets and expand production capacity in existing markets.

The use of FDI to strengthen export strategies can include investments in research and development, sales and marketing, and operations. By entering into an FDI agreement in another country, a company can take advantage of the local market conditions, economic structure, and regulatory environment to improve some aspects of their business operations. This could potentially include developing newer, more efficient technology, gaining access to new distribution channels and markets, as well as relocating certain aspects of the production cycle. Examples of FDI export strategies include setting up research and development centers, leveraging distribution and sales networks, and establishing production facilities.

Mergers and acquisitions are another form of international expansion and export strategy. M&A transactions involve one company acquiring or merging with another, commonly employed when a company seeks to acquire the talents and skills of the target company or seeks to benefit from other synergistic opportunities. Companies targeting potential M&A opportunities in order to export need to ensure a comprehensive analysis of the target company and its potential future benefits. It is essential to also consider potential cultural differences between the companies and the potential for political instability or delays in the regulatory environment.

FDI and M&A strategies can be extremely powerful tools to help multinational companies build and expand operations in international markets. While both strategies require different approaches and considerations, they each have their own advantages and pitfalls. Companies should carefully consider the available opportunities and strategies in order to best serve their export strategies needs.

International Strategic Alliances and Joint Ventures

The utilization of international strategic alliances and joint ventures has become an increasingly popular way for companies to increase their market share and enhance the quality of their products and services. Companies can leverage global markets in order to expand their reach, access new technologies, or enhance logistic networks -all of which can benefit the bottom line. The process of forming a strategic alliance can not only help a business to expand globally but also offers several benefits when attempting to enter the export market.

One of the main benefits of international strategic alliances and joint ventures is increased access to global markets. Companies often form alliances or joint ventures with local companies in order to gain access to their native markets. This can be especially useful for companies that are interested in entering smaller or developing markets where local expertise is essential. Additionally, such alliances offer companies the chance to tap into potential sources of new customers, partners and suppliers.

Moreover, international strategic alliances and joint ventures can help companies to access new technologies. A alliance or joint venture can provide a company access to innovations and knowledge that would otherwise be difficult to obtain. This can be especially important in the export market where foreign markets may offer superior technologies, better access to the latest developments, and insights that can offer advantages over competitors. Further, new technologies can lead to cost savings and other efficiencies, which can often be a deciding factor in entering the export market.

Finally, forming strategic alliances and joint ventures can often provide a company with access to improved logistics and transportation networks. Access to these networks can enable a company to better manage their export operations and distribution. Such networks can provide greater access to customers, reduce delivery times, and lower costs -all of which can be important factors involved in entering the export market.

International strategic alliances and joint ventures are an important tool that can help companies improve their standing in the export market. In order to be successful, however, companies must ensure that they carefully assess potential partners and do due diligence to secure the best possible deals. Careful planning and evaluation can go a long way to ensuring that a company's global ambitions are fulfilled.

CHAPTER ELEVEN

International Trade Agreements and Tariffs

International trade agreements and tariffs are an essential part of export businesses. Trade agreements between countries provide the framework for exports, imports and investments. Tariffs, on the other hand, are fees placed on goods and services moving across international borders. As such, these two factors are critical components of an export business and play an important role in the economic development of countries.

Trade agreements reduce or eliminate tariffs and other barriers to commerce, and they often include regulations that encourage investment and production. These agreements come in various forms, such as free trade agreements, comprehensive economic and trade agreements, and bilateral agreements. In free trade agreements, countries agree to reduce or eliminate barriers to trade, such as tariffs and quotas. In comprehensive economic and trade agreements, countries agree to reduce or eliminate tariffs, non-tariff trade barriers, and other restrictions that hinder the flow of goods and services across borders. Bilateral agreements are agreements between two countries that provide for the mutual reduction of trade barriers.

Tariffs are taxes or charges imposed by one country on imports from another. They are used to raise revenue for the government, to equalize the cost of goods traded, to protect domestic industries from international competition, or to punish countries for violating certain regulations. Tariffs are typically assessed on a per-unit basis, meaning that the higher the quantity of goods being imported, the higher the tariff. For example, a country may choose to impose an ad valorem tariff, which means that the tariff amount is based on the value of the goods.

Tariffs are a form of protectionism, and they can have a significant impact on an export business. Tariffs increase the cost of imported inputs, making it more expensive to produce goods. Additionally, tariffs raise the price of imported goods, making them less competitive in the global market. For these reasons, it is essential that export businesses be aware of and fully understand the tariffs imposed by foreign countries on their products.

In summary, international trade agreements and tariffs play a key role in export businesses. While they are used to reduce trade barriers and encourage investment, they can also increase the cost of producing goods and reduce competitiveness in the global market. It is therefore essential for export businesses to understand the agreements and regulations that apply to their industry and to assess the potential impact of tariffs on their exports. Understanding the implications of these two factors is critical for success in the export business.

CHAPTER TWELVE

Government Regulations and Compliance

Exporting goods and services overseas can be an incredibly lucrative business opportunity, and yet international companies attempting this endeavor must also wrestle with various governmental regulations and compliance related factors. For any successful export business, there is no substitute for understanding and adhering to the rules, regulations and standards governing international trade.

Depending on the country of origin, the goods and services being exported, and the destination, governments may impose different laws, restrictions, formalities and procedures. It is critical to correctly determine the applicable standards and follow them closely, and to take time to learn the international trade laws and the norms of the country to which the goods are being shipped.

One of the fundamental elements of compliance is recordkeeping. Export businesses must maintain accurate and detailed records of any transaction involving the exporting of goods and services. This should include relevant paperwork, invoices, and related documents. Additionally, it is essential to understand the requirements for tariffs and licenses, obtain any necessary permits, and be aware of proper documentation for cargo shipments. A proper licence may be necessary in order for the company to operate in a given country, depending on the laws of the origin country, or upon the terms of international treaties between the two countries.

Some export businesses seek professional assistance to help them navigate the compliance minefield. Legal advisors and customs brokers are invaluable in helping companies manage their export operations in an effective and compliant manner. Consulting firms can provide further guidance on addressing issues with foreign customs jurisdictions.

It is important to remember that regular reviews of operations should be conducted by qualified individuals to ensure ongoing compliance with applicable regulations and laws. This includes making sure the particulars on the product labels meet applicable regulations and that all governmental agencies involved in the trade are properly acknowledged and respected. Furthermore, diligent attention should be paid to changing international laws and tariffs, to ensure the business stays abreast of any changes that may affect compliance.

Understanding and respecting governmental regulations and compliance factors are critical elements of any successful export business. Taking the time to become educated on all applicable regulations, obtain the required permits and licenses, maintain the necessary paperwork and records, and continuously review operations to remain mindful of changing laws and standards, will help ensure companies maximize the power and potential of their business.

CHAPTER THIRTEEN

Legal Issues in Export Management

Export management, the procedure that documents, facilitates, and supervises the international shipment of goods or services, is an increasingly complex area of business subject to legal compliance. Legal issues in export management are diverse, and organizations must stay abreast of the ever-evolving legal landscape to ensure they remain compliant.

One of the primary issues organizations must be conscious of is knowing the country's export regulations. This includes, among other things, understanding the export controls within countries and determining the licensing requirements of goods and services. Organizations must ensure goods and services are not being shipped in violation of a country's export regulations.

Organizations must also be aware of sanctions, embargos, and boycotts that can impede the normal flow of goods and services. Depending on the location the goods and services are being exported from and to, the laws can be drastically different and organizations must be sure it is compliant with the laws of both countries. Companies must also be aware of money laundering laws and regulations, especially if money is being moved across borders. Particularly stringent anti-money laundering regulations must be strictly enforced.

Organizations also need to be cognizant of international rules of trade or "rules of origin", which determine where goods and services originate from, as this can affect tariff structures and other legal requirements. Furthermore, organizations must be aware of the different customs and regulations when it comes to international shipping requirements, terms of payment, and the transfer of personnel.

Beyond the legal regulations, organizations should also be aware of any industry standards, codes of conduct, or ethical considerations that are relevant to their business. By familiarizing themselves with local industry or trade norms, organizations can ensure that proper export management procedures are being followed and allow for more efficient operations.

At face value, legal issues in export management are complex and can appear daunting. However, with proper evaluation, education, and compliance, organizations can ensure legal obligations are met without any disruption to their export operations. By having an informed understanding of the legal compliance involved in export management, organizations can successfully conduct business in a growing and ever-evolving global market.

Ethics and Social Responsibility in Export Management

Export management involves a myriad of different stakeholders on both the home and international front. As such, it is essential that those working in the export management field ensure they are upholding the highest ethical and social standards in their operations.

First, any responsible export manager needs to understand their local and international legal obligations, as well as moral commitments. These include human rights, competition laws, and labor laws, among many others. It is the responsibility of the export manager to ensure that their actions are compliant with relevant international standards and laws; they should take the time to become thoroughly familiar with applicable regulations and be vigilant in ensuring their own behavior and the behavior of those they work with are in accordance with them.

Importantly, a sense of ethical responsibility to the

environment must be present in any export management plan. This includes planning for sustainable practices in the production of goods and materials, as well as environmental considerations in the actual transport of the goods from country to country. It is essential that the export process is conscious of its environmental footprint and works towards reducing it.

The social implications of export management must also be considered. Of utmost importance is the notion that export operations must be conducted without taking advantage of or exploiting vulnerable populations. Export management should remain sensitive to the social implications of their operations and structures, making sure that the economic foot-print left by these activities does not disproportionately burden any one group within a given society. In addition, the export manager should strive to provide balanced and mutual benefit to both the home and receiving countries.

Ethical and social responsibility are essential aspects of any responsible export management plan. This involves understanding and adhering to legal obligations, ensuring environmental sustainability, and striving for social evenness in their activities. It is only through the proactive implementation of these standards that export management can be conducted responsibly and sustainably.

CHAPTER FIFTEEN

Identifying and Entering New Markets

Identifying and entering a new market in export business can be an exciting and potentially rewarding journey. However, the process is often fraught with difficulty as there are a number of factors to consider and numerous challenges to overcome. In order to be successful, it is essential to go through a thoughtful process that takes into account the complexities that come with doing business in a new country or region.

The first step to entering a new export market is to identify markets that offer potential. Companies looking to enter new export markets should do comprehensive market research to identify the most attractive and viable opportunities. This should include a detailed analysis of the external economic and political environment, the competitive landscape, and the market trends. Understanding the cultural dynamics is also important in order to better ascertain the appetite for the company's products and services. Once the most promising markets have been identified, companies should conduct further analysis to better understand the needs and trends of potential customers.

Following the market research phase, companies should select the best market opportunity that fits their goals and capabilities. Before any resources are committed to entering the new export market, a thorough risk assessment should be completed. This includes a comprehensive analysis of the potential risks associated with entering the specific market, such as political and economic risks, and the potential for failure. Risk assessments should also include an analysis of the cost of entry, competitor activity, and the potential for success.

Once an export market has been identified and the risks assessed, companies should undertake a series of activities to prepare for market entry. These include obtaining the necessary permits, establishing local presence, and finding adequate financing to get the operation off the ground. Companies should also explore ways to reduce the cost of operations and expenses related to international expansion.

Finally, companies should select the most appropriate strategy for entering the new market. Depending on the size and complexity of the export project, companies may choose to use their own resources, hire a third-party intermediary, or use a mix of both. It is also important to define the roles and responsibilities of each party. This will ensure that each team has a clear understanding of their obligations and that the project is conducted in an efficient and effective manner.

By implementing a step-wise approach to market entry and following best practices, companies can identify and enter new export markets with greater confidence and reduce the risks associated with doing business outside their own borders. In doing so, companies can unlock the immense potential of international expansion and reach new heights of success in their export ventures.

Building and Managing International Relationships

Effective international relationships are essential for companies who want to export products and services across the world. A key challenge many companies face is identifying how to go about building and managing these relationships. This essay will discuss how building and maintaining international business relationships is important in export business, and will outline the various strategies companies can use to establish and maintain these relationships.

The first step in building and managing international relationships is to identify potential customers and partners. Companies should research the markets they are targeting to understand the cultural and economic factors, as well as assess the needs of those markets. This helps companies identify the best strategies to enter global markets, as well as where future growth opportunities may exist. Companies should also consider forming joint venture partnerships with other companies in the target market, as this can help them gain access to local resources and networks, as well as increase their market share.

After identifying potential partners, companies should develop a plan for maintaining those partnerships. Companies should strive to build relationships of trust and respect with potential customers and partners. This can be done by exchanging information and offering support and guidance, as well as communicating regularly and staying up to date on their partner's individual needs. Companies should also take a proactive approach to solving problems quickly and effectively while ensuring their partners feel they are valued.

Communication is another key factor in building and managing international relationships. Companies should communicate clearly and frequently with their partners and customers, as this can help build trust and ensure that both parties are on the same page. Companies should also seek to develop a common understanding of expectations and objectives, as this can help ensure that the relationship is mutually beneficial.

Furthermore, companies should make sure to invest in their partners and customers. This can involve helping their partners access resources they need, offering free training to help their partners use the product or service, or providing incentives to customers. Companies should also focus on providing value to their partners or customers in order to maintain loyalty.

Finally, companies should take a long-term approach to

building and managing international relationships. Companies should strive to build long-term relationships with their partners and customers that are based on mutual respect and trust. This can involve taking steps to ensure the relationship is mutually beneficial, as well as committing to ongoing communication and customer service.

Building and managing international relationships is an important component of success in the export business. It is essential for companies to take the necessary steps to ensure they are effectively engaging with partners and customers in order to create long-term, mutually beneficial relationships. By using the strategies outlined above, companies can set themselves up for success in the global market.

CHAPTER SEVENTEEN

Intellectual Property and Trademark Protection

Intellectual Property (IP) and Trademark Protection are essential for companies engaging in export business. Intangible assets such as IP and trademarks can be a significant source of competitive advantage in volatile international markets, but without effective protection, companies can quickly find their innovations replicated and their brands undermined. Companies looking to export their offerings need to understand the full scope of their IP and TM protection in order to maximize their market chances and safeguard their competitive capabilities.

First and foremost, companies need to determine their IP portfolio. This includes trademarks and patents, which offer strong protection from the unauthorized replication of innovations, products, or services. IP protection of this kind can be acquired in the location where a company's export activities are based, or even outside the territory. Companies must also seek to register their trademarks in any jurisdiction they expect to export to, to help ensure their products and services stand out in international markets.

Companies should be aware that some patent or trademark applications may be rejected, or their contracts may be unenforceable in today's increasingly globalized market. Companies should thus seek specialized legal advice to understand their local and foreign protection options and any loopholes they can use to bolster their legal standing.

Outside of intellectual property protection, export companies need to ensure they take the necessary steps to protect their brand image and prevent copycat products from being released by competitors. This can be achieved through strategic marketing, maintaining exclusive distribution networks, controlling pricing, and carefully controlling pricing and other elements of a company's international brand positioning.

To enable these steps to be taken more effectively, companies should also consider enlisting a third-party in their export strategy. A professional marketing advisor can provide valuable insights into market conditions, competitive landscape and more. Furthermore, a dedicated IP lawyer (or a consultancy working on the company's behalf) can be appointed to help protect the company's trademarks, identify potential infringement issues and analyze local laws to determine the best protection strategy.

When done properly, IP and TM protection will ensure companies can export their IP and TMs with confidence and make the most of their competitive advantages in the international markets. Additionally, companies can minimize the risk of their IP or TMs being replicated by competitors, or their resources being exploited. All in all, a long-term commitment to protecting IP and TMs is key to the success of international business.

CHAPTER EIGHTEEN

Foreign Exchange and Currency Risk Management

Export business requires careful managing of foreign exchange and currency risks to ensure the ongoing success of the business. By understanding and mitigating risks that come along with international trading, businesses can reduce the uncertainty of export operations.

Currency risk or foreign exchange risk arises from fluctuations in foreign exchange rates. As the currency markets are highly volatile and unpredictable, export businesses must understand and prepare to respond to these changes. Exchange rates can have a major effect on a company's costs and income and can therefore take a toll on its bottom line. Businesses must have a sound strategy and approach to foreign exchange management to minimise the risks associated with the operations.

When starting export business operations, it is important to consider the economic policies of the countries involved.

Nations implement policies regulating the value of currency and therefore a business must be prepared to respond to changes that may arise. Additionally, political actions and events should be monitored as they may bring abrupt changes to currency exchange markets and require businesses to adapt their approaches. Companies must also review other financial market developments such as global inflation or rate of interest.

Aside from concerning the currency exchange rates, businesses must also be aware of regulations and other policies that must be met, such as transfer pricing and taxation arrangements. These policies can affect the business's foreign exchange management needs. Additionally, businesses must consider the other parties of the transaction to ensure that the amount of foreign currency required is accurately calculated and that the business is not exposed to unnecessary risks.

To manage foreign exchange risk, businesses may decide to hedge against currency fluctuations with financial instruments. Forward contracts and options, for instance, can be used to lock in currency levels at a certain time in the future. Businesses can also choose to donate currency to offset any losses due to foreign exchange fluctuations.

Finally, in addition to strategic foreign exchange risk management, businesses must also remain mindful of their own operating costs. For instance, engaging in foreign currency transactions can incur high transfer fees and other costs that should be accounted for.

Export businesses must be aware of and prepared to

respond to the risks associated with foreign exchange and currency markets. By incorporating effective policies and measures into the business operations, companies will be able to successfully minimise the profitability and profitability risks in the international marketplace.

CHAPTER NINETEEN

Export Financing and Insurance

Export financing is a set of financial instruments designed to enable and encourage international trade. This type of financing generally focuses on growing markets, allowing businesses to better understand and accommodate a new region's trading environment. Export financing and insurance can help minimize the risks and costs that are associated with trading across borders. Through this type of financing and insurance, businesses can access the resources necessary for successful international trade in a structured, organized and safe environment.

Export financing typically includes various forms of short-term finance, export credit and foreign exchange services. This financing helps protect a business from potential risks associated with international trade, such as nonpayment, currency exchange rate fluctuations and unfair competition. Export credit insurance can be used to cover the buyer's risk of nonpayment and cover political risks such as non-delivery, war and terrorism.

In order to facilitate effective export financing and

insurance in export management, it is important to be aware of the different services available. Export credit insurance is a critical part of international trade as it can help protect exporters from potential losses due to buyer payment defaults. It is typically provided by either an insurance company or a bank as a value-added service for their clients. Export financing and insurance should be tailored to meet the needs of the particular export market and all available options should be considered when selecting insurance and financing solutions.

When managing the export financing process, companies should ensure that there is strong communication between the exporter, the buyer and the financier, as well as clear and consistent procedures for vetting credit applications and making payments to suppliers. Companies also need to ensure that all international regulations are respected and kept in mind when making payments and verifying the identities of their buyers and suppliers.

Export financing and insurance can provide a valuable source of financing and protection to companies that are engaging in international trade. Through the use of both financing and insurance, businesses can experience more security when trading across borders and have better control over their cash flow and credit exposure. However, it is important to be aware of the risks associated with this type of financing, as well as have a good understanding of all available services. By utilizing the right financing and insurance tools, companies can minimize potential risks and maximize their international trade activities.

CHAPTER TWENTY

Quality Control and Standards

Quality control and standards are essential components in the export business management industry. Quality control and standards involve the processes, standards, and practices that help a company maintain a consistent and safe level of service and product. It is not limited to just quality but includes the integrity of the products and services, safety, timeliness, and packaging. Quality control and standards also ensure that the products or services are compliant with applicable regulations, as well as free from non-compliance or defects that would lead to a customer's dissatisfaction or cause harm to customers.

The export business management industry needs to have quality control and standards in place to ensure that risks are managed and minimized. It is important for export companies to be able to identify and resolve concerns and issues before they become a problem. Quality control and standards should be specified before implementation and continual improvement should be continually monitored and reviewed.

Export business management companies must use quality control and standards that are aligned with their global business objectives. Quality control processes should be developed to assess the quality of any finished product or service, while standards should be applied to production operations, materials and products, machinery, and processes. Quality standards should also be applied to suppliers, to ensure that they meet the company's stated requirements.

Quality control and standards should be consistently maintained throughout the entire export process. Each phase of the process should be monitored and evaluated to ensure that the product is correctly designed and manufactured, meets the specified quality and safety standards, is packaged correctly, and can be exported or imported safely and efficiently. Furthermore, all staff should be trained in the use of quality control and standards and all procedures should be documented.

It is important to ensure that quality control and standards are up-to-date, which can be achieved by carrying out regular reviews, both internally and with independent quality assessment teams. Regular reviews also provide an opportunity to gain customer feedback on the product/ service and identify areas for improvement.

Quality control and standards are essential components of export business management. Quality control and standard processes should be designed to meet the needs of global businesses, all staff should be trained in their use, and reviews should be continually conducted to ensure everything meets stated quality and safety requirements.

CHAPTER TWENTY-ONE

Logistics and Supply Chain Management

Logistics and supply chain management play an integral role in export businesses. For an effective coordination of all related material, information, and financial activities, careful management of the logistics process is essential for successful export sales. Many companies have come to rely on logistics and supply chain management to provide their customers with quality products at a minimal cost and in the shortest timeframe possible.

The export business encompasses many aspects, from determining customer needs and fielding customer inquiries, to planning and anticipating demand. This is where logistics and supply chain management come in. A reliable supply chain system should track the entire process, from starting production to delivering the finished product. This includes ensuring that raw materials and supplies reach the right supplier, that packaging and labeling are accurate, and that orders are shipped according to schedule. The goal is to avoid any delays that could cause customer dissatisfaction and customer loss.

Logistics and supply chain management are also important for ensuring the safe transport of goods. This can involve ensuring that cargo is stored properly and that appropriate transport is used to ensure that it reaches its destination on time and without being damaged. A reliable and robust logistics and supply chain management system should also be able to predict potential issues before they arise, helping to reduce losses due to damages or delays.

Finally, logistics and supply chain management are also key for managing import and export regulations. The import and export of goods is governed by a variety of laws and regulations, and it can be difficult for exporters to keep up with the constantly changing landscape. A reliable supply chain system should help to manage these regulations, ensuring that shipments remain compliant.

Logistics and supply chain management play an essential role in the export business. With careful management and an effective system, companies can ensure that their customers receive quality products in a timely manner, while also adhering to all import and export regulations. Logistics and supply chain management are key components of any successful export business.

CHAPTER TWENTY-TWO

E-commerce and Online Marketing

The world of business has seen a massive shift in the last twelve years, due to the introduction of e-commerce and online marketing. Companies that were once confined to their respective geographical regions or countries, have now been able to reach a global audience thanks to these two advancements. It is now easier than ever for businesses to engage in export business management, in order to increase their customer base and grow their profits.

E-commerce is a term used to describe the buying and selling of goods over the internet. It has revolutionized the way in which businesses are able to transact and communicate with potential customers. By having an online presence, companies can easily reach customers from different countries and better manage the global market. This helps to minimize costs associated with exporting, as goods are now able to be purchased and sold electronically. Moreover, implementing e-commerce opportunities for export business management helps to reduce time lost due to customs and shipping, making the process much more efficient.

Despite the numbers of benefits associated with e-commerce, it is also important to consider how online marketing can be used to promote export business management. Online marketing is an effective way of advertising goods and services to a global audience. By utilizing various platforms such as social media and search engine optimization, businesses can successfully target those interested in their products. Additionally, the use of digital marketing tools such as email campaigns and paid advertising can help to promote a business's products and services to the right people.

E-commerce and online marketing have become essential components of export business management. By creating an online presence, companies are able to penetrate new markets and reach a global customer base. Furthermore, online marketing is also beneficial, as it helps to further promote a business's products and services in an effective manner. Therefore, embracing these technologies is a sure fire way for a business to greatly increase its profitability, and achieve success in the export market.

CHAPTER TWENTY-THREE

Export Management in Emerging Markets

Today, exports play a major role in the international business world, as companies look to tap into new markets and growth opportunities. As traditional markets become saturated, many firms are turning to emerging markets to capture new sources of sales and profits. But managing exports in these new and ever-evolving markets can be a challenge.

Export management in cmerging markets refers to the strategies, tactics, and systems used to effectively manage and grow exports in these markets. It involves an understanding of local economies and trade regulations, knowledge of market nuances and trends, and leveraging technology to maximize efficiency.

The first step in export management is to understand the political and economic landscape in emerging markets. Companies must address questions such as the economic condition of the country, currency fluctuations, and regulations around tariffs, taxes, and shipping. Gaining an in-depth knowledge of these political and economic challenges can help firms develop strategies to identify and capitalize on market opportunities.

Next, it's important to conduct market research to assess demand, pricing dynamics, distribution channels, and any unique local customs. This helps firms create tailored marketing campaigns to maximize returns in their target markets. Additionally, it's important to assess the competition and how to differentiate from them.

In addition to physical market research, it can also be beneficial to gain insights from the digital landscape. Companies should be leveraging data analysis and insights from online platforms to gain further intelligence about emerging markets, allowing them to hone their focus and make smarter decisions on where to allocate resources.

Finally, for successful export management, companies must integrate technology solutions. Technology can make exporting more efficient, from managing inventory and forecasting to order fulfillment, shipping, and payment processing. It's also important to ensure that technology solutions are tailored to work within the regulations of local governments.

Export management in emerging markets requires a unique combination of skills and solutions. By taking the time to understand the political and economic landscape, perform market research, and leverage technology solutions, companies can streamline their exporting processes and maximize profits in these new markets.

CHAPTER TWENTY-FOUR

Export Management in Developed Markets

Exporting is the process of sending out products and services from one country to another without the expectation of receiving anything in return. Export management involves the management of the activities involved in selling products and services abroad and the oversight of associated activities such as the handling of documents and the managing of transportation costs. Export management in developed markets is essential for gaining competitive advantage in international markets.

The first step in successful export management is market research. Market research helps entrepreneurs identify potential customers and competitors, as well as understand the target market. This research helps business owners determine the right products and services to export. Market research also helps entrepreneurs understand the changes in customer demands, the competitive environment and the regulations of the country in which the products or services are being exported.The second step is to develop a comprehensive export strategy. This includes deciding on the type of products or services to export, the target customers, the countries that should receive priority focus, the pricing strategy and how the products or services will be distributed. By establishing an export strategy, entrepreneurs can maximize their export opportunities with the quickest return on investment.

The third step is to select the proper export channels. Exporting can be done either directly or through intermediaries. Direct exports require the company to take full responsibility for the entire sales process, while intermediaries simplify the process by already having existing relationships with customers, distributors and other markets. Depending on the complexity of the product or servicE, as well as the desired markets and customers, companies must determine which option is appropriate.

The fourth step is to manage all trading activities. Companies must ensure that all contractual and regulatory requirements are met, and all transactions are monitored to ensure accuracy. This requires extensive paperwork and the management of shipping, freight and customs issues. Once products have left the country of origin, export managers must ensure customs declarations, licenses and inspections are handled in a timely manner.

The fifth step is to evaluate results and adjust accordingly. Companies should track the performance of international sales and adjust their strategy as needed. By monitoring performance, companies can identify areas for improvement, adjust pricing and distribution strategies and determine whether additional resources are required to meet the demands of the market.

Export management in developed markets is essential for gaining a competitive edge. Through the coordination of market research, developing a comprehensive strategy, selecting the appropriate export channels, managing all trading activities and evaluating results, companies can maximize their success in international markets. By utilizing export management tools and leveraging the latest technologies, businesses can position themselves for international success.

CHAPTER TWENTY-FIVE

Case studies and Success stories in Export Management

The story of successful export management starts long before the goods and services enter the market abroad. Expertise in export management requires a thorough understanding of the complete range of procedures and implications, from the source of goods and services to the international market. Those who understand the process and manage it effectively can reap the rewards in terms of improved profits, customer satisfaction, and market presence.

Export management typically involves a wide variety of functions, such as product identification and selection, pricing, promotions, transportation, international and domestic marketing, compliance with laws and regulations, financial management, and export documentation. An effective export management strategy relies on expertise in the above disciplines, and must recognize and act upon any political, economic, cultural, and market conditions that may affect it.

Case studies and success stories in export management say that in order to effectively handle operations, product pricing must be determined to ensure a good return on expenses and optimize market presence. Export managers must develop comprehensive strategies for marketing goods and services for export, including pricing not only for a given product but also for its competition. Market intelligence such as historical trends, current events, and customer preferences must be sourced through various channels and interpreted to adjust strategies accordingly.

Promotional campaigns must also be considered, wherein reaching the right audience with appropriate messaging is the goal. A good export management team must be familiar with the current trends and expectations of a target market, as well as the competition in the export sector in order to craft effective and attractive campaigns. Export financing is another important component that requires oversight, ensuring that the exporter is able to access the same type of financing options available to domestic firms, when needed.

Effective international laws and regulations must be monitored to ensure compliance, from the export of goods and services to customs requirements, labeling, product identification, and other due considerations. Non-compliance can prove to be costly for an export management team, involving reparations for legal disputes or stalled shipments.

Successful case studies in export management show that

expertise in the above processes and activities are critical for export success. The export of goods and services to foreign markets involves a number of complexities that can be managed effectively and efficiently with the appropriate level of planning, foresight, and market intelligence. Those companies that recognize these challenges and dedicate resources to the task of developing a comprehensive export management strategy can experience the rewards of expansion into global markets.

Other Books Of The Author

1. The Moments When I Met God
2. Kashiyile Theertha Pathangal
3. GURU GYAN VANI
4. Abhiprerak Gita
5. ASSI SE JAIN GHAT TAK
6. Hopelessness of Arjuna
7. The Soul and It's True Nature
8. Sense of Action (Karma)
9. Action through Wisdom
10. Action through Wisdom
11. THEORY AND PRACTICAL OF EVERY ACTION
12. LOGICAL UNDERSTANDING OF THE SUPREME
13. THE IMPERISHABLE SUPREME
14. Yatra Nishadraj se Hanuman Ghat Tak
15. Yatra Karnatak Ghat se Raja Ghat Tak
16. Yatra Pandey Ghat se Prayagraj Ghat Tak
17. Yatra Ranjendra Prasad Ghat se Dattatreya Ghat Tak
18. YaatraSindhiya Ghat se Gwaliar Ghat Tak
19. Yatra Mangala Gauri Ghat se Hanuman Gadhi Ghat Tak
20. Yatra Gaay Ghat Se Nishad Ghat Tak
21. MAA GANGA, GHATEN EVM UTSAV
22. Ganga Arti Dev Deepavali evam Any Utsav
23. Potentials of Digitalized India
24. VEDIC CONSCIOUSNESS
25. A Brief Introduction to Vedic Science
26. Kashi ke Barah Jyotirling
27. IMPACT OF MOTIVATION
28. Let's have a Milky Way Journey
29. Color Therapy in a Nutshell

59. The Holistic Cow: A Look at the Physical, Spiritual, and Cultural Importance of Cows in India
60. Arts of Healing
61. Exploring the Divine
62. Understanding Five Elements
63. The Etymology of Ram
64. Symbols of India
65. Voice of Change (About Speeches of Great Men)
66. She Speaks (About Speeches of Great Women)
67. Patriotism on Celluloid – Brief About Patriotic Films
68. The Music of Motivation: A Brief Guide to Inspirational Film Songs
69. **Unlocking the Secrets of the Dashopanishads**
70. A Cultural Mosaic
71. Ancient Traditions, Modern Minds
72. Ecos of Ancient Wisdom
73. Beneath the Surface
74. From Temples to Ashrams
75. Sages of the Subcontinent
76. The Art of Healling (Ayurveda, Yoga & Naturopathy)
77. Indian Kitchen
78. The Festivals of India
79. The Indian Epics Retold
80. The Power of Mantras
81. The Indian River Ganges
82. The Indian Architecture
83. Rites of Passage
84. The Indian Silk Road
85. The Indian Literature
86. The Indian Villages
87. The Indian Folks & Crafts
88. The Way of Buddha
89. The Ramayan of Tulsidas

121. Innovative Startups - 25 Startup Ideas to Spark Your Business Creativity
122. Export Management: Strategies for Global Success
123. Exporting from India - A Step by Step Guide
124. Finance Fundamentals: Mastering Financial Management for Business Success
125. Global Growth Strategies for International Business Development
126. Marketing Mastery: Unlocking the Secrets of Modern Marketing
127. Operations Mastery: Managing the Flow of Value in Business
128. Strategic Business Management: Navigating the Modern Business Landscape
129. Human Resource Management Strategies for Building and Managing a High Performance Team

Contact

DR. JAGADEESH PILLAI

MBA & PhD in Vedic Science

Four Times Guinness World Record Holder

Winner of Mahatma Gandhi Vishwa Shanti Puraskar and Global Peace Ambassador

Gemology, Astro & Vastu Consultant - Spiritual Counselor

Consultant for designing World Record Ideas

Efficient Tarot Card Reader

9839093003

myrichindia@gmail.com

drjagadeeshpillai@facebook

drjagadeeshpillai@instagram

jagadeeshpillai@youtube

www. JAGADEESHPILLAI.com

|| LOKAHA SAMASTHAHA SUKHINO BHAVANTU ||